THE FUTURE SPLIT OF PAKISTAN

THE PRESENT ECONOMIC CRISIS OF PAKISTAN ARE VERY SERIOUS

ISHWAR SINGH

I am dedicating this book to those innocent peoples who lost thier lives during the partition of India.

Contents

Foreword

Ishwar Singh have more than ten years of experience in writing and in research activities. He is a tremendous writer. He is doing excellent job by writing about "The Future Split of Pakistan". He had shown very keen interest in the field of Political Science and other cultural issues.

He is also a very excellent teacher and also having deep knowledge about the Social Science issues. I have always seen him working very hard for his various books. He just want to express about the Indian culture to our new generations in a simple and brief manner. I wish him all the very best for his new book.

Birinder Pal Kaur

Preface

This book actually talk about the demand of various independent countries in Pakistan. How Pakistan is struggling to counter this opposition from various groups.

I think you will enjoy this book and engage yourself in a thorough reading.

Acknowledgements

Writing a book is harder than I thought and more rewarding than I could have ever imagined. None of this would have been possible without my best friend, my teacher, my best motivator, my beloved mother Amarjit Kaur. She was the first who inspired me for my goals and taught me various subjects and created my interest specially in Social Sciences. She stood by me during every struggle and all my successes. Whatever I had achieved in my life it is due to my mother.

I'm eternally grateful to my father Pal Singh, who took in an extra mouth to feed when he didn't have to. He taught me discipline, tough love, manners, respect, and so much more that has helped me succeed in life. I truly have no idea where I'd be if he hadn't given me a roof over my head whom I desperately needed at that age.

To my father-in-law Narinder Singh for their moral support during the up and downs in my life. He taught me how to live positive even in the worst situations by sharing his personal experiances. He is the man who suggest me to write a book in your life because it will be your book by which you will be remembered in future.

To Himanshu Jena, Thakur Sandeep Singh, Yashpal Sharma for their motivational support during my book writing days. To Shashi Bala Minocha for giving their extraordinary support specially for good Preface writing.

CHAPTER ONE

The Future Split of Pakistan

The very well known country in the world which is also known as a hub to produce world class terrorists to disrupt the world peace. Yes I am here talking about our neighbor country Pakistan. Pakistan, the country which was founded on the eve of bloodshed in Punjab and Bengal was earlier described by Mohammad Ali Jinnah as the idol country for the purpose of development in South Asia. Oh yes, he was right. He had established such a country which is really a rare model of development in the South Asia. But what are the categories of development by Pakistan?

These are the state funding model of terrorism, a debtor with very less money in their foreign exchange reserves, no money to pay salary to their diplomats in various countries, continues freedom struggle by baloch people, political instability from the day of independence and so many government assets are ready for sale to chinese and US companies.

Pakistan turned into hooked up in 1947, from the partition, as a country for Muslims. The using pressure in the back of the Pakistan Movement have been the Muslims withinside the Muslim minority provinces of United

Province (present day Uttar Pradesh) and Bombay Presidency as opposed to the Muslims from the Muslim majority provinces. Its formation turned into primarily based totally on the idea of Islamic nationalism.

As a part of the Partition of India in 1947, Bengal turned into partitioned among the Dominion of India and the Dominion of Pakistan. The Pakistani a part of Bengal turned into referred to as East Bengal till 1955 and thereafter as East-Pakistan following the implementation of the One Unit program. However, rampant corruption in the ranks of the Pakistani authorities and bureaucracy, financial inequality among the country's wings induced specially with the aid of using a loss of consultant authorities and the authorities's indifference to the efforts of fierce ethno-nationalistic politicians, like Sheik Mujibur Rahman from East Pakistan, who fought for Bangladeshi independence, ended in civil battle in Pakistan and next separation of East Pakistan because the People's Republic of Bangladesh. Bilateral family members among the 2 wings grew strained over the shortage of reliable reputation for the Bengali language, democracy, nearby autonomy, disparity among the 2 wings, ethnic discrimination, and the imperative authorities's vulnerable and inefficient remedy efforts after the 1970 Bhola cyclone, which had affected hundreds of thousands in East Pakistan. These grievances caused numerous political agitations in East Bengal and in the end a combat for complete independence.

There are separatist moves in Pakistan that are primarily based totally on ethnic and nearby nationalism, which include independence moves in Balawaristan,Sindh and Balochistan. The authorities of Pakistan has tried to subdue those separatist moves.

The separatist motion in Balochistan is engaged in a low-depth insurgency towards the Government of Pakistan.

In 2009, the Pew Research Center carried out a Global Attitudes survey throughout Pakistan, wherein it puzzled respondents whether or not they considered their number one identification as Pakistani or that in their ethnicity. The pattern protected a place representing 90% of the grownup populace, and covered all predominant ethnic groups. According to the findings, 96% of Punjabis diagnosed themselves first as Pakistanis, as did 92% of Pashtuns and Muhajirs; 55% of Sindhis selected a Pakistani identification, even as 28% selected Sindhi and 16% on "each equally"; while 58% of Baloch respondents selected Pakistani and 32% on their ethnicity and 10% selected each equally. Collectively, 89% of the pattern opted their number one identification as Pakistani.

Similarly in 2010, Chatham House carried out an opinion ballot withinside the Pakistani and Indian-administered areas of Kashmir asking respondents in the event that they favoured independence or an accession to both countries; in Azad Kashmir managed through Pakistan, 75% of respondents voted to enroll in Pakistan, 4% voted for independence, and 1% voted for accession to India, even as in Jammu and Kashmir (state) administered through India 85% voted to enroll in Pakistan. In the northern vicinity of Gilgit-Baltistan, longstanding neighborhood sentiments oppose any merger of the location with Kashmir, and alternatively call for a constitutional integration with Pakistan.

The ballot carried out amongst citizens of Jammu and Kashmir administered through India and Azad Kashmir administered through Pakistan additionally indicates a polarization in opinion, 71% of the populace stated they could vote for the entire of Kashmir to enroll in Pakistan even as 25% stated they could vote for it to be independent.

The Baloch Liberation Front (BLF) separatist organization become based via way of means of Jumma Khan Marri in 1964 in Damascus, and performed an crucial position withinside the 1968-1980 insurgency in Pakistani Balochistan and Iranian Balochistan. Mir Hazar Ramkhani, the daddy of Jumma Khan Marri, took over the organization withinside the 1980s. The Balochistan Liberation Army (additionally Baloch Liberation Army or Baluchistan Liberation army) (BLA) is a Baloch nationalist militant secessionist organisation. However, Jumma Khan Marri ended his competition and pledged allegiance to Pakistan on 17 February 2018. The said dreams of the organisation encompass the status quo of an impartial kingdom of Balochistan become independent from Pakistan and Iran. The call Baloch Liberation Army first have become public in summer time season 2000, after the organisation claimed credit score for a chain of bomb assaults in markets and railways lines. The BLA has additionally claimed obligation for the systematic ethnic genocide of Punjabis, Pashtuns and Sindhis in Balochistan (approximately 25,000 as of July 2010) in addition to blowing up of fueloline pipelines. Local Balochs have additionally been centered via way of means of the separatist companies withinside the province. Brahamdagh Khan Bugti, alleged chief of Baloch Liberation Army (BLA), additionally requested separatists to behavior ethnic cleaning of Non-Baloch residents from the province. In 2006, the BLA become declared to be a terrorist organisation via way of means of the Pakistani and British governments.

However, the insurgency led via way of means of the Baloch separatists withinside the province is on its closing leg. Baloch separatists were dropping their leaders and that they were not able to fill their ranks. There is likewise presently ongoing infighting among the exceptional insurgents companies. The closing rebel chief, Balach Marri, become capable of hold the exceptional rebel companies united. However, after his dying in Afghanistan, infighting broke out among diverse rebel companies. The insurgents had been not able to update him. Similarly, Baloch separatist comply with Marxism. However, the Marxism ideology died the world over and there's no different ideologies to prevail it. So the founder of Baloch separatist are dead. Moreover, assaults on pro-authorities leaders and politicians who're inclined to participate in election has additionally contributed to the decline in separatist appeal.

The News International said in 2012 that a Gallup survey carried out for DFID discovered that almost all of Baloch do now no longer aid independence from Pakistan. Only 37 percentage of Baloch had been in favour of independence. Amongst Balochistan's Pashtun populace aid for independence become even decrease at 12 percentage. However, a majority (sixty seven percentage) of Balochistan's populace did favour extra provincial autonomy. Majority of Baloch additionally do not aid separatist companies. They aid political events who use legislature to deal with their grievances. Experts additionally declare that maximum of the nationalists withinside the province had come to consider that they may combat for his or her political proper inside Pakistan.

As of 2018, the Pakistani kingdom become the use of Islamist militants to overwhelm Balochi separatists. Academics and reporters withinside the United States were approached via way of means of Inter-Services Intelligence spies, who threatened them now no longer to talk approximately the insurgency in Balochistan, in addition to human rights abuses via way of means of the Pakistani Army, otherwise their households could be harmed.

Sindhudesh is an concept of a separate Homeland for Sindhis proposed via way of means of Sindhi nationalist events for the advent of a Sindhi state, which might be unbiased from Pakistan. The motion is primarily based totally withinside the Sindh area of Pakistan and turned into conceived via way of means of the Sindhi political chief G. M. Syed. A Sindhi literary motion emerged in 1967 below the management of Syed and Pir Ali Mohammed Rashdi, in competition to the One Unit policy, the imposition of Urdu via way of means of the imperative authorities and to the presence of a massive range of Muhajir (Indian Muslim refugees) settled withinside the province.

However, neither the separatist celebration nor the nationalist celebration have ever been capable of take centre degree in Sindh. Local Sindhis strongly guide Pakistan People Party (PPP). The unprecedented and unhindered fulfillment of the PPP in Sindh indicates the choice of Sindhis for a constitutional political method over a separatist time table to remedy their grievances. Similarly public opinion is likewise now no longer closely in favour of those events either. In different words, neither the Sindhi separatists nor the nationalists have tremendous famous guide — genuinely now no longer the sort as a way to lead them to able to fuelling a full-scale insurgency. Almost all the Sindhis have a sturdy Pakistani identification and like to stay a part of Pakistan.

In 2012, a Sindhudesh rally turned into organised via way of means of a nationalist celebration in Karachi, which had a substantially low turnout. The nationalist celebration had claimed that they might accumulate round million humans for his or her million march. Although, handiest 3,000 to 4,000 humans attended the rally.

In 2020, the Pakistani authorities banned a couple of separatist clothes which includes the Jeay Sindh Qaumi Mahaz - Aresar group, Sindhudesh Liberation Army, and Sindhudesh Revolutionary Army.

An independence motion presently exists in Gilgit-Baltistan (called "Balawaristan" through its supporters). Balawaristan National Front (BNF-H) led through Abdul Hamid Khan had been seeking to searching for independence of Gilgit-Baltistan from Pakistan. However, Abdul Hamid Khan unconditionally surrendered to Pakistan safety officers on eight February 2019. Following his surrender, 14 greater participants of BNF-H had been arrested for his or her anti-Pakistani activities. Since then the destiny of BNF-H is unknown. Another corporation through the call of Balawaristan National Front led through Nawaz Khan Naji seeks to claim Gilgit-Balistan an self sustaining Region below Administration of Pakistan until Promised pelbicite.

In Pakistani facet of Kashmir, no political events with separatist inclinations can take part withinside the elections. All events in Pakistan's Kashmir and Gilgit-Baltistan ought to receive that Kashmir is a part of Pakistan and joined Pakistan below what the Pakistani government recall an accession agreement. Because of this, best pro-Pakistani nationalist events are capable of win the elections, as others are barred. Furthermore, maximum of the forms and civil provider is managed through the significant authorities, with the "Kashmir council", that's headed through the Prime Minister of Pakistan. Pakistan made in addition movements to manipulate the place through having the vicinity divided into Gilgit-Baltistan and Azad Kashmir regions. In addition, Pakistani government took away the vicinity's unique popularity and ruled through the significant authorities in Pakistan, much like India, which Pakistani government condemned.

Sardar Arif Shahid, turned into a Kashmiri nationalist chief who recommended the independence of Kashmir from each India and Pakistan's rule. He turned into killed on May 14, 2013 outdoor his residence in Rawalpindi. It turned into the primary time any pro-independence Kashmiri chief turned into centered on this manner in Pakistan. His supporters allege that he turned into killed through Pakistan safety forces. Within the place, "Custodial torture and intimidation of independence supporters and different activists" has occurred.

In 2010, Chatham House, a London primarily based totally assume tank, did a survey, subsidized through Saif al-Islam Gaddafi, in each Pakistani and Indian administered Kashmir. Based on a pattern length of 3,774, it located that Kashmiri's on each facets desired independence. The survey states, 44% of Kashmiri's in Pakistan administered Kashmir desired independence.

In October 2019, the People National Alliance organised a rally to loose Kashmir from Pakistani rule. As a end result of the police seeking to prevent the rally, a hundred human beings had been injured.

Jinnahpur refers to an alleged plot in Pakistan to shape a breakaway self reliant kingdom to function a hometown for the Karachi primarily based totally Urdu-talking Muhajir community. Mohajirs are immigrants who got here to Pakistan from India withinside the wake of the violence that observed the independence of India in 1947. The alleged call to accept to the proposed breakaway kingdom was "Jinnahpur", named after Mohammed Ali Jinnah. In 1992, the Pakistani army claimed it had observed maps of the proposed Jinnahpur kingdom withinside the workplaces of the Mohajir Qaumi Movement, notwithstanding the party's robust denial of the authenticity of the maps. Despite the party's robust dedication to the Pakistani kingdom, at that point authorities of Nawaz Sharif selected to apply it as the premise for the army operation towards the MQM, called Operation Clean-up.

The Muhajir Sooba is a political motion which seeks to symbolize the Muhajir human beings of Sindh. This idea floated as a political bargaining device through the chief of Muttahida Qaumi Movement, Altaf Hussain for the introduction of a Muhajir province for the Muhajir-majority regions of Sindh, which might be unbiased from Sindh authorities.

Pakistan is a growing with a semi-commercial economic system. Primary export commodities encompass textiles, leather-based goods, sports activities equipment, chemicals, and carpets/rugs.

The increase poles of Pakistan's economic system are located alongside the Indus River; the diverse economies of Karachi and fundamental city centres in Punjab, co-current with lesser advanced regions in different elements of the united states of america. The Pakistani economic system has suffered withinside the beyond from inner political turmoil, a hastily developing population, and combined degrees of overseas funding. Foreign change reserves are strengthened via way of means of constant employee remittances, however a developing cutting-edge account deficit—pushed via way of means of a widening exchange hole as import increase outstrips export expansion—should draw down reserves and hose down GDP increase withinside the medium term. Pakistan is presently present process a technique of monetary liberalization, which includes the privatization of all authorities corporations, that is geared toward attracting overseas funding and lowering finances deficits.

As of May 2021, the Pakistani authorities has anticipated that destiny increase fees might be five percentage—one of the maximum in South Asia. According to the World Bank, the degrees of poverty in Pakistan fell from 64.three percentage in 2001 to 21.nine percentage in 2018. The united states of america's enhancing macroeconomic function has led the Moody's Investors Service to improve Pakistan's debt outlook to "stable".

In 2017, Pakistan's GDP (PPP) crossed US$1 trillion. In 2021, the expected GDP (PPP) stood at US$1.33 trillion. Current account deficit is one of the demanding situations that the united states of america's economic system is dealing with after hikes withinside the costs of global commodities. By May 2019, the Pakistani rupee had passed through a yr-on-yr depreciation of 30 percentage vis-à-vis the USA greenback. 2020 noticed the start of Phase 2 of the China–Pakistan Economic Corridor, with new billion-greenback agreements.

Pakistan external debt is now near about US $109 Billion, which converted the Pakistani economy into an unsustain situation. To run the country and to fulfill all the expenses, Pakistan needs more money as loan. Pakistani government is already ready to sale out Pakistan International Airlines and Pakistani Railways to multinational companies either belongs to USA or China. Very soon the major government companies may be under the hands of foreign companies. In case of India, Modi government also sale out Air India to Tata group but here the buyer is Indian and that's the difference. Pakistani army general also requested to US President Joe Biden to ask IMF to support us. Pakistan's foreign exchange reserve is also draining and it is not possible for Pakistan to continue their import for a longer time. If Pakistan will continue with such situations then there are much more chances for the split of Pakistan. According to my prediction Pakistan can no longer exist after 2060 and can be split into various independent countries.

Printed by Libri Plureos GmbH in Hamburg, Germany

9 798888 059623